E
178
A9
v.8

Athearn, Robert

The American heritage
new illustrated history
of the U.S.

WITHDRAWN

DATE DUE

JUN 21 '78			
DEC 10 '80			
MAR 7 '84			
APR 26 '95			
JUN 16 '95			

JUN 17 '81
OCT 15 '81

A Civil War version of the U.S.O. provides in one building (top picture) a place for soldiers to shave (left), eat (center), and wash clothes (right).

COVER: *The first Union advance at Winchester on September 19, 1864, was bungled, but Philip Sheridan rallied his men for this final victorious charge.*

FRONT ENDSHEET: *A militia regiment from New York, dressed in blue coats and red trousers, prepares for inspection in an 1861 painting by James Walker.*
COLLECTION OF ALEXANDER McCOOK CRAIGHEAD

CONTENTS PAGE: *This painted panel is one of four from Lincoln's private railroad car. One of the others shows a Washington portrait, two are landscapes.*
JOSLYN ART MUSEUM

BACK ENDSHEET: *Some of Lee's soldiers fold their flag for the final time. Many Southern regiments burned or buried their flags rather than surrender them.*
COLLECTION OF ALEXANDER McCOOK CRAIGHEAD

*"A knowledge of the past prepares us for the crisis
of the present and the challenge of the future."*

JOHN F. KENNEDY
From his special foreword in Volume 1

THE AMERICAN HERITAGE
NEW ILLUSTRATED HISTORY
OF THE UNITED STATES

VOLUME 8
THE CIVIL WAR

By ROBERT G. ATHEARN
Professor of History, University of Colorado

CREATED AND DESIGNED BY THE EDITORS OF
AMERICAN HERITAGE
The Magazine of History

PUBLISHED BY
DELL PUBLISHING CO., INC., NEW YORK

CONTENTS OF THE COMPLETE SERIES

Foreword by JOHN F. KENNEDY
Introduction by ALLAN NEVINS
Main text by ROBERT G. ATHEARN

A COMPLETE INDEX FOR ALL 16 VOLUMES APPEARS IN VOLUME 16

CONTENTS OF VOLUME 8

CHAPTER 22

THE WAR COMES

The Confederate bombardment of Fort Sumter sparked a great military conflagration that was to blaze in America for four bitter, bloody years.

In the days following Sumter's surrender, President Abraham Lincoln called for 75,000 volunteers, declared a naval blockade of Southern ports, and ordered a special session of Congress. These events electrified the North and sent thousands of young men scurrying to the recruiting offices. Reaction in the South was much the same. Virginia, Arkansas, North Carolina, and Tennessee soon joined the seven states that had formed the Confederate States of America. Southerners answered the call to the colors as enthusiastically as Northerners.

Neither side expected a long war. Northern boys were called up for 90 days—plenty of time, it was thought, to crush the "insurrection." Southerners were equally optimistic, anticipating a quick march on Washington to dispose of Lincoln and the "Black

The drummer boy, youngest of the soldiers on both sides in the Civil War, seems forlorn and lost as he stands in a barren camp in this Julian Scott painting.

Republicans." Both armies were little more than collections of state militia, thrown together with the idea of delivering one hammer blow and then returning home for the fall harvest.

As harried officers tried to whip some semblance of order and discipline into these raw levies, Lincoln turned his attention to the crucial and wavering border states of Maryland, Missouri, and Kentucky. Rioting broke out in Baltimore and St. Louis, with Union troops and civilians fighting in the streets, but vigorous and hard-handed action by the federal government kept both Maryland and Missouri from seceding. Confederate President Jefferson Davis and Lincoln played a cat-and-mouse game with Kentucky, each hoping the other would shatter the state's precarious neutrality. Eventually Northern troops got the upper hand, and Kentucky, too, remained in the Union.

The nation's attention quickly focused on Washington and Richmond, the two capitals, just 100 miles apart. Members of Congress pressed the army to advance on Richmond. Army officers were anxious also, for the 90-day enlistment period was drawing to

The 6th Massachusetts Regiment was on its way to Washington on April 19, 1861, traveling through Baltimore, when it was attacked by Southern sympathizers.

a close. Old Winfield Scott, whose army service dated back to the War of 1812, was in charge of the military preparations. He appointed Brigadier General Irvin McDowell to lead the assault on the Confederate force at Manassas, 25 miles southwest of Washington. McDowell protested to the President that his troops were far from ready for a fight. "You are green, it is true," Lincoln replied, "but they are green also. You are all green alike."

On July 21, 1861, the two armies clashed near a little stream called Bull Run. McDowell's thrust was at first successful. Then his attack fell apart in the face of stiffening resistance, and the Federals withdrew toward Washington. The retreat became a rout, but the Southern troops were too disorganized to follow up their victory.

Bull Run threw the North into a state of shock. It was hard to believe that Union troops had met with such a reverse. Angered and determined, the North began to reorganize its forces. McDowell was replaced by young, self-confident Major General George B. McClellan, who already had won a series of small victories in

COLLECTION OF ALEXANDER MCCOOK CRAIGHEAD

western Virginia. When General Scott retired in November, McClellan replaced him as general-in-chief of the Union Army. McClellan was a first-rate organizer and drillmaster, and during the winter his Army of the Potomac began to assume the look of a real fighting force. There were many in the North who still felt one more battle would put an end to the rebellion.

Real war begins

The new year of 1862 began auspiciously for the Union. A series of victories in the Western theater demolished the Confederate defense line that ran from Cumberland Gap in the Alleghenies to the Mississippi River. On January 19, Brigadier General George Thomas won a fight at Mill Springs to wrest eastern Kentucky from the Confederates. On February 6, an obscure brigadier general named Ulysses S. Grant, cooperating with a fleet of gunboats under Flag Officer Andrew Foote, captured Fort Henry on the Tennessee River.

Within a week, Grant had laid siege to Fort Donelson, 12 miles away on the Cumberland River. When the Con-

Jefferson Davis is in the center of this anonymous painting, with four of the Southern military leaders—Beauregard, Jackson, Stuart, and Johnston.

federate commander requested surrender terms, Grant replied bluntly, "No terms except an immediate and unconditional surrender can be accepted." Fort Donelson and its 15,000 defenders gave up on February 16, and the entire center of the Confederate defense line was gone. At once the taciturn man from Illinois became known as Unconditional Surrender Grant, and the North had a new hero.

The Richmond government desperately rallied its forces to try to regain the initiative in the Mississippi Valley, an area it could not afford to lose. General Albert Sidney Johnston assembled a striking force at Corinth, Mississippi, just below the Tennessee border, and looked for a chance to launch a counterattack.

He soon found it. Grant had advanced up the Tennessee River as far as Pittsburg Landing, where he encamped his army near a little country meetinghouse called Shiloh Church to await reinforcements. At dawn on April 6, Johnston struck hard at the unwary Federals. By nightfall the Confederates had pushed Grant's army almost into the river. But the Federals received reinforcements, and the next day Grant's counterattack drove the enemy back to Corinth.

The Battle of Shiloh was fought by soldiers largely untrained but fiercely determined, and the casualty lists—more than a third of the 77,000 men engaged were shot, with General Johnston among the dead—stunned both North and South. Hopes for a quick and comparatively bloodless end to the war died among the peach blossoms at Shiloh.

Federal forces in the West kept up the relentless pressure. The Mississippi River stronghold of Island Num-

ber 10 fell to Union troops, and a brief, savage naval battle featuring ironclad gunboats opened the river as far south as Memphis, Tennessee. As the Confederates apprehensively looked northward, Flag Officer David G. Farragut's powerful squadron battered its way past the forts guarding New Orleans and on April 25 gobbled up the largest city in the Confederacy. The South's hold on the great river was soon reduced to the 250 miles between the citadels of Port Hudson, Louisiana, and Vicksburg, Mississippi.

While these important victories were being won in the West, McClellan (whom the newspapers had nicknamed the Young Napoleon) was having his troubles in the East. Pressure was exerted upon him from every side to advance on Richmond. He had no capacity for understanding the political aspects of a civil war, and he soon had

NATIONAL ARCHIVES

George B. McClellan

McClellan was in charge of the unsuccessful advance on Richmond made in 1862. He is shown below riding at the head of his staff, surveying the camp set up for the campaign on the Pamunkey River in Virginia.

Entered according to Act of Congress
in the Year 1885 by the
McCORMICK HARVESTING MACHINE CO.
in the Office of the
Librarian of Congress at Washington.

BATTLE OF SHIL

THE "McCORMICK" MACHINES COME VICTO

PRESENTED WITH COMPLIMENTS OF

This print of the Battle of Shiloh is of the area where the fighting was so fierce that it was

·APRIL 6ᵗʰ 1862·

I. General Grant and Staff

COPIED BY SPECIAL PERMISSION
From The
·PANORAMA PAINTING·
ON EXHIBITION IN CHICAGO

IF EVERY CONTEST, AND WITHOUT A SCRATCH.

RVESTING MACHINE COMPANY

later referred to as the Hornet's Nest. Grant and his staff are on the mound at the right.

much of official Washington on his neck. In March, 1862, he was goaded into action.

McClellan rejected the direct overland route to Richmond; instead, he ferried his army down Chesapeake Bay and landed it at the tip of the Virginia Peninsula. His idea was to advance the 70 miles to Richmond with Union naval forces on the York and James Rivers protecting both flanks. To appease President Lincoln, he left 40,000 troops to protect Washington—troops he expected to join him when he laid siege to Richmond.

Lee takes a command

It took the cautious general two months to get within sight of the Confederate capital. The rebels under General Joseph E. Johnston fell back until May 31, when Johnston counterattacked at Fair Oaks. The two-day battle was indecisive, but one result was to have a far-reaching effect on the Civil War. Johnston was seriously wounded, and President Davis appointed General Robert E. Lee to command in his place.

Lee had been generally considered the best officer in the United States Army, and General Scott had offered him command of the main federal forces after Fort Sumter. It was an agonizing decision, but the Virginian chose to follow his state out of the Union. He served as Davis' military adviser until the Confederate President put him in command of the Army of Northern Virginia. Lee would lead

T.S.C. Lowe's federal observation balloon was used to study the rebel battlefields.

it until the Battle of Appomattox.

Even before he took command, Lee had conceived a strategy to prevent the federal reinforcements in the Washington area from descending on Richmond from the north as McClellan advanced from the east. The instrument of that strategy was General Thomas Jackson, a former professor at the Virginia Military Institute who had won his nickname of Stonewall at Bull Run and who was proving to have a positive taste for war.

Jackson's small force slipped into the Shenandoah Valley and began to upset the Washington government.

Federal units (including McClellan's reinforcements) descended on Jackson from all sides. His answer was one of the dazzling campaigns of the war. "All Old Jackson gave us was a musket, a hundred rounds, and a gum blanket, and he druv us like hell," one of his men said. Within a month he won five battles, tied up more than 50,000 Union troops, and then slipped away to join Lee at Richmond.

Lee now took the offensive. In the Seven Days' Battles he repeatedly attacked McClellan's force and drove it all the way across the Virginia Peninsula to the James River. Lee could never quite bring the Federals to a decision, but McClellan was a beaten

McClellan's vast train—4,300 wagons and ambulances—fords Bear Creek near Savage's Station on the harassed retreat of the Union forces from Richmond.

man, his only thought being to save his army.

McClellan blamed his defeat on the politicians in Washington, but Lincoln chose not to debate with his general over what might have been. Instead, he turned to the Western theater and brought to Washington two generals who, he hoped, would get the war back on the right track. To replace McClellan as general-in-chief, he installed a fussy, bookish soldier named Henry Halleck, known irreverently in the regular army as Old Brains. To command a new field army composed of the troops around Washington and the parts of McClellan's force being evacuated from the peninsula, the President chose pompous, opinionated John Pope. (Pope seems to have been one of the few men Robert E. Lee actively despised. Pope, Lee ordered, was to be "suppressed.")

Lee hastened to strike before McClellan's troops could be firmly joined with Pope's. Stonewall Jackson slipped around Pope's flank with half of the Confederate Army and led the Union general a chase until he let himself be brought to bay on the old Bull Run battlefield. Meanwhile, the other wing of Lee's army, under James Longstreet, was stealthily approaching. Jackson beat off Pope's determined attacks on August 29, but when Pope renewed the assault the next day, Longstreet sprang the trap and sent the Federals into headlong flight. John Pope had indeed been suppressed. He was sent off to fight Indians and McClellan got his army back.

The Second Battle of Bull Run left angry disgust in the minds of the hard-war wing of the Republican Party, a clique known as the Radicals. They needed a scapegoat, so they descended on General Fitz-John Porter, whom Pope accused of disobeying a battle-field order. (The order had been impossible to obey; Porter was aware of Longstreet's presence even if Pope was not. But that made no difference

Dejected Yankee soldiers survey a row of boxcars burned to their trucks by Stonewall Jackson in his raid on Pope's supply base at Manassas Junction.

to the Radicals.) Senator Zachariah Chandler of Michigan wondered why Pope had ever let Porter leave the battlefield alive after such cowardice in the face of the enemy. Senator Benjamin "Bluff Ben" Wade of Ohio was already on record as saying that generals should never even consider retreat, adding that if the soldiers could not win a victory, they ought to come home in their coffins.

As a result of all this, Porter, a good fighting general with the wrong political connections, was railroaded out of the army. Wade's notorious Joint Committee on the Conduct of the War gained new strength. It would plague President Lincoln until the war was over, and strike fear into the hearts of his generals.

Southern high tide

Lee determined to keep the initiative, and he launched an invasion of the North. McClellan wrote his wife, "Again I have been called upon to save the country," and set out in cautious pursuit. At the same time, in the Western theater, Braxton Bragg's Confederate Army of Tennessee drove headlong into Kentucky, thrusting for the Ohio River. For the only time in the Civil War, the South was making a coordinated effort to invade and subdue the North. The fall of 1862 was to mark the high tide of the Confederacy.

With James E. B. "Jeb" Stuart's cavalry screening his advance from the Yankees, Lee slipped into the Shenan-

Stonewall Jackson

doah Valley. Half the Confederate Army was detached to seize the Union garrison at Harpers Ferry, astride Lee's line of communications. But now fate stepped in to give McClellan a helping hand: An Indiana corporal stumbled on a lost copy of Lee's orders that had been wrapped around three cigars. McClellan realized he was closer to the parts of Lee's army than they were to each other. But he did not move quite fast enough. Lee pulled together his scattered forces in a precarious position on the banks of Antietam Creek near the hamlet of Sharpsburg, Maryland.

McClellan was a superb military housekeeper, and the men of the Army of the Potomac loved him as they loved no other of their numerous commanders. But in the heat of battle

Burnside, by taking more than three hours to cross a bridge over an easily forded stream, seriously delayed the Union thrust at the Battle of Antietam.

something went out of him. On September 17, the Federals repeatedly attacked Lee's lines, and by the narrowest of margins repeatedly failed to break through. "The sun seemed almost to go backwards," a rebel soldier wrote. "It appeared as if night would never come."

Antietam was a bitterly fought battle, and it cost more men killed and wounded—some 23,500—than any other single day in the Civil War. McClellan could not nerve himself to throw in his reserves for one final blow, and the battle was a standoff. Lee aggressively held his battered army in its lines for another day, then retreated across the Potomac River

into Virginia. One wing of the Confederate invasion had failed.

In the West, however, the Union had a crisis to face, and it was the legacy of Old Brains Halleck. After Grant's victory at Shiloh, Halleck stepped in to gather up the fruits. But he made war by the book. He scattered his immense forces far and wide, garrisoning captured territory and rebuilding railroads, and the Confederates were given time to recuperate. Braxton Bragg neatly slipped the leash Union General Don Carlos Buell was holding and headed for the Northern heartland. Bragg was nearly to Louisville before he turned off to install a secessionist government in the Kentucky capital of Frankfort. As a result, Buell got between the Southerners and the Ohio River.

The two armies finally stumbled into each other near the town of Perryville, Kentucky, on October 8. It was a strange battle, with neither commander apparently aware of what was going on. Like Antietam, Perryville was indecisive; and like McClellan, Bragg seemed to lose his grip in the test of combat. He gathered up his forces and tramped back to Tennessee.

Although Antietam and Perryville were not military victories for the Union, they did stop the South's drive into the North and cut Southern hopes for foreign intervention, based upon its successful campaigns. Also, after Lincoln announced the Emancipation Proclamation, broadening the conflict into a struggle to free the slaves, the possibility of foreign support was further hindered.

To Europe, and particularly to England, the outbreak of war in the United States had seemed to spell opportunity. For years some Britons had watched with anxiety as America grew in commercial and industrial importance, and as the major users of Southern cotton, they resented the high tariff walls that kept them from trading their manufactures for it. If the aristocratic classes of Great Britain and France had their way, the Confederacy might have received direct military aid.

Southern agents worked long and hard to bring this about. After the Emancipation Proclamation, however, Britain's middle classes and workers, with all liberals and humanitarians, clearly saw the Civil War as a struggle to end slavery. A civilized power could hardly go to war for a cause that endorsed human bondage, or actively support it. The South's dream of foreign intervention now guttered out like a candle in a windstorm.

Stalemate

Two weeks after Antietam, McClellan was still in Maryland, suffering from what Lincoln described as "the slows." While the Union commander temporized, Jeb Stuart's troopers rode completely around his army on a reconnaissance. This was the sort of exploit that the hard-fighting, flamboyant Stuart loved (he had done it before, on the Virginia Peninsula), and understandably the people of the North were furious. Lincoln's patience was exhausted, and he made a clean sweep: McClellan was out and Major General Ambrose Burnside was in as commander of the Army of the Potomac; in the West, William S. Rosecrans replaced Buell—he, too, had the slows—as head of the Union Army of the Tennessee.

Burnside honestly protested that he was not up to the job, but he dutifully moved southward to the Rappahannock River opposite Fredericksburg. There he sat waiting for the belated arrival of his pontoon bridges while Lee efficiently fortified the heights behind the town. At last Burnside crossed the river, and on December 13, 1862, launched a massive frontal attack on the rebel lines.

Up the incline moved waves of blue-clad soldiers, stubbornly facing the flaming Confederate guns and being slaughtered like cattle. As the attackers slipped in the blood of their comrades and stumbled over fallen bodies, the rebels watched in awe. George Pickett, to find immortality the following year at Gettysburg, wrote his wife that the "brilliant assault . . . was beyond description. Why, my darling, we forgot they were fighting us, and cheer after cheer went up all along our lines."

It was a brutal, senseless kind of bravery—that of men following their orders in an ill-conceived attack upon a well-entrenched enemy. Burnside lost 13,000 men, Lee fewer than 5,000. When the awful facts of this debacle came home to the people in the North, confidence in the Lincoln administration waned and attacks on the President reached new heights. Senator Wade's Joint Committee on the Conduct of the War rose to new paroxysms of fury, for it had hoped to establish Burnside as its latest hero. On January 25, 1863, Lincoln removed Burnside and replaced him with Major General Joseph Hooker. He was the Army of the Potomac's fifth commander in a year and a half of fighting.

In Tennessee, Rosecrans began a drive to capture Chattanooga, gate-

After the defeat at Fredericksburg, Burnside and his men went up the Rappahannock under such foul conditions that the move was called the Mud March.

*The Mississippi made a loop at Vicksburg, and Grant set his men to digging
canals in an attempt to divert the river and so bypass the city's defenses.*

way to the Deep South. At Murfreesboro he found his way blocked by Bragg. On December 31, both commanders planned to hold with their right wing and attack with their left; had they carried this out, the two armies might have turned around each other as if caught in a gigantic revolving door. But Bragg struck first and bent the Union force back on itself. Rosecrans rallied, and on January 2, 1863, won back his lost ground. Each army lost about a quarter of its strength; neither was in condition to resume the contest for six full months.

Two new generals and two new battles, and the Union was no closer to victory. The ever-growing casualty lists seemed to testify that the Northern cause was stalled on dead center. And along the Mississippi River, as the weeks of the new year passed, it appeared that Unconditional Sur-

render Grant, too, had struck a stone wall trying to subdue Vicksburg.

The turning point

The great Confederate fortress was perched on a bluff overlooking a bend in the Mississippi, impregnable to attack from the river. The swampy character of the terrain made it hard for Grant even to find dry ground from which to launch an attack on the land side. Through the winter of 1862–63, he and his lieutenant—red-haired, volatile William Tecumseh Sherman—tried and rejected one scheme after another to get at the citadel. The Federals dug canals and cut levees and made channels through bayous, and at one point nearly lost Rear Admiral David Dixon Porter's gunboat squadron in a watery maze.

In April, 1863, Grant finally perfected a daring plan. He marched his

army down the Louisiana side of the river opposite Vicksburg. Porter sped his fleet of gunboats and transports past the thundering Vicksburg batteries on the night of April 16 and ferried Grant's force across the river below the city. If Grant's campaign failed, the vessels would be stuck there, for they were too under-powered to beat their way upstream again past the batteries.

To solve the supply problem, the Union soldiers were ordered to live off the country, although they were outnumbered and deep in enemy territory. Grant proposed to isolate the Vicksburg garrison before it could be reinforced by Confederate units

from central Mississippi. In a whirlwind campaign reminiscent of Stonewall Jackson's effort in the Shenandoah Valley the previous year, he won five battles in less than three weeks, severed Vicksburg's lifelines, and besieged the city.

In Virginia meanwhile, Hooker was moving against Lee's Army of North-

James Walker's painting records the charge of A.P. Hill's rebels on the first day at Gettysburg. Hill's men have overrun the Union line on McPherson's Ridge. Eventually the federal troops were outflanked and driven back to a last-stand position around the seminary building in the middle distance. At the left, in the distance, are Culp's and Cemetery Hills, and at the right, the Round Tops—all important Union posts on the next days.

651

ern Virginia. He said he hoped God would have mercy on General Lee, "for I will have none." But Lee liked to pick his own places to fight, and he chose a tangled woodland along the Rappahannock River west of Fredericksburg known as the Wilderness. Hooker had not intended to fight there, and his grand plans began to evaporate in the clouds of battle smoke that enveloped the crossroads hamlet of Chancellorsville.

Outnumbered two to one, Lee gambled once more—and won. He gave Jackson half his force and sent him off on a long flanking march. In the late afternoon of May 2, Jackson struck the Union right flank and crushed it. In four more days of heavy

George Gordon Meade

Nearly the entire battlefield at Gettysburg is shown in James Walker's paint-ing of the final day. General Meade is visible just right of center, mounted, with field glass. Below, the Union forces, in the rain, pursue Lee's army.

fighting, Lee pinned the Army of the Potomac against the Rappahannock. When he turned and routed a relieving force, the whole Union army pulled back across the river. Chancellorsville was Lee's most brilliant victory, but it was a costly one. Stonewall Jackson was mortally wounded, shot accidentally by his own men. Lee mourned, "I have lost my right arm."

In the frantic hope of forcing Grant to give up his siege of Vicksburg and bring his army east, Lee now initiated a gigantic raid against the North. He divided his veteran army into three corps, under James Longstreet, Richard Ewell, and A. P. Hill, and raced through the Shenandoah Valley and into Pennsylvania. Hooker shadowed him skillfully, but he had clearly lost the confidence of President Lincoln. On June 27, Major General George Gordon Meade, a capable and irascible veteran, took command of the Army of the Potomac. Just four days later, on July 1, advance elements of both armies collided at the Pennsylvania market town of Gettysburg. The greatest battle of the Civil War had begun.

The first day of Gettysburg was a decided victory for Lee, who was able to pour more men into the widening battle than Meade. The Federals were driven through the town to a fishhook-shaped area of high ground. Its shank was known as Cemetery Ridge. On July 2, Lee made heavy assaults on both ends of this line, but the tough and seasoned Army of the Potomac

beat them off, often in the most brutal hand-to-hand fighting.

The climax of the battle came the next day, July 3, when 15,000 rebels under George Pickett lined up for a frontal assault on the Union center. (At this moment, far to the west, Grant and Confederate General John Pemberton were discussing the surrender of the Vicksburg garrison.) Pickett's columns surged forward and briefly breached the Union center, but Meade's men hurled them back.

These fateful days in July, 1863, sealed the doom of the Confederacy. On July 4, Vicksburg capitulated, soon to be followed by Port Hudson 250 miles downriver. As Lincoln said, "The Father of Waters goes unvexed to the sea." The Confederacy was split in two. On July 5, Lee set his mangled army on the roads back to Virginia, his 17-mile-long wagon train of frightfully wounded men leaving a trail of shocked horror through the once peaceful countryside. Desperately hurt men swamped Gettysburg and nearby towns, and a Quaker nurse admitted, "There are no words in the English language to express the suffering I have witnessed today."

But one man was able to give expression to it, and also to the Civil War's ultimate meaning. In November, at the dedication of the Gettysburg military cemetery, a tall, ungainly man from the Illinois prairie spoke for all "the brave men, living and dead," who had fought, and were to fight, on the battlefields of that war.

MEMORIAL HALL LIBRARY, ANDOVER

PRESIDENT LINCOLN

Lincoln, in his message to Congress on December 1, 1862, said, "Fellow-citizens, *we* cannot escape history. We of this Congress and this administration will be remembered in spite of ourselves. No personal significance, or insignificance, can spare one or another of us. The fiery trial through which we pass will light us down, in honor or dishonor, to the latest generation." It is almost exactly in the sense that Lincoln stated that we remember the Civil War and particularly his place in it. The war was the beginning of a conflict we are still trying to resolve, in the North and the South, as we attempt to honor the equality this country promises. Today, Lincoln is seen as the embodiment of that struggle, and he is remembered as a man who fought and died to preserve the Union and make equality live for all.

655

IN WASHINGTON

At Lincoln's first inauguration on March 4, 1861, the Capitol dome was still a half-completed shell and Lincoln an untried politician who had taken on some of the most complex responsibilities any American President had faced. In fighting to restore the Union, he had little time for anything but the great struggle that as President he had officially begun, and few moments like the imagined one at the left. The engraving shows his wife Mary, two sons—Robert, in uniform, and Tad—and a portrait of Willie, a son who had died at the age of 12. Below is one of the few social events during the war— a reception held for Ulysses S. Grant, who stands to the left of the President.

COLLECTION OF WINSLOW CARLTON—FRANCIS G. MAYER

LINCOLN
IN CARTOONS

Few Presidents have been the subject of so many cartoons, but few have had a physical appearance so easily caricatured and have been involved in questions about which such controversy raged. At the left, Lincoln, dressed as the all-powerful knight under whose foot is the Constitution, the law, and habeas corpus, contemplates a paper marked Defeat. Below, in a symbolic 1862 painting by D. G. Blythe, Lincoln, chained to strict constitutional behavior by Tammany Hall Democrats, is handicapped in his efforts to destroy the fierce dragon of rebellion.

To a French cartoonist, Lincoln appears so powerful in his own country that he holds Uncle Sam in his hand and looks at him through a magnifying glass. To the left and below are two comments on Lincoln's election victory in 1864: Long Lincoln becomes even longer, and a giant Majority carries him through the election waters.

THE ACHIEVEMENTS

Although what Lincoln accomplished as President was largely related to the Civil War, it was such a crucial part of America's history that his deep involvement only certifies to his greatness. The symbolic painting at the upper left shows his attempt at reconciliation between the North and the South. At the left, Lincoln reads the Emancipation Proclamation to his cabinet on July 22, 1862. The document was important in rallying the North's support of the war, but it also took a stand for the Union against the injustice of slavery. Above is a painting of the delivery of the Gettysburg Address, by Fletcher C. Ransome. The speech lasted but a few minutes, and only later was it recognized as the great statement of the principles of the Union. At the right is Lincoln at City Point, Virginia, being welcomed by his troops and by the liberated slaves. The North's victory was in no small measure a result of his leadership.

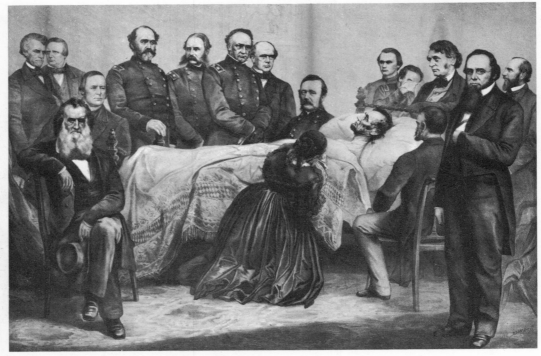

THE MURDER

On April 14, 1865—Good Friday—John Wilkes Booth, an actor then 26, entered Ford's Theatre, where Lincoln and his wife were watching a play titled *Our American Cousin.* He went to Lincoln's box just as the President's bodyguard left to get a drink. Booth opened the door quietly, stepped into the box, and shot Lincoln in the back of the head (left). In a matter of seconds, Booth was on a horse he had waiting at the stage door. Lincoln did not live long; he died the next morning (left, bottom). The search began for the murderer and his co-conspirators, with a $100,000 reward offered (right). On April 26, Booth, who had injured his leg, was shot as he moved toward the door of a barn that had been set on fire by cavalrymen who had found him (below).

SURRAT.   BOOTH.   HAROLD.

War Department, Washington, April 20, 1865,

$100,000 REWARD!

THE MURDERER

Of our late beloved President, Abraham Lincoln,

IS STILL AT LARGE.

$50,000 REWARD

Will be paid by this Department for his apprehension, in addition to any reward offered by Municipal Authorities or State Executives.

$25,000 REWARD

Will be paid for the apprehension of JOHN H. SURRATT, one of Booth's Accomplices.

$25,000 REWARD

Will be paid for the apprehension of David C. Harold, another of Booth's accomplices.

LIBERAL REWARDS will be paid for any information that shall conduce to the arrest of either of the above-named criminals, or their accomplices.

All persons harboring or secreting the said persons, or either of them, or aiding or assisting their concealment or escape, will be treated as accomplices in the murder of the President and the attempted assassination of the Secretary of State, and shall be subject to trial before a Military Commission and the punishment of DEATH.

Let the stain of innocent blood be removed from the land by the arrest and punishment of the murderers.

All good citizens are exhorted to aid public justice on this occasion. Every man should consider his own conscience charged with this solemn duty, and rest neither night nor day until it be accomplished.

EDWIN M. STANTON, Secretary of War.

TRIBUTE
AND TOLL

Lincoln's funeral cortege was a spectacle that reaffirmed his importance to the nation. His body was taken from city to city on the way to Springfield, Ohio, where it was buried. Below, the procession passes through New York City. At the left, Lincoln is posed beside Washington, over the words "The Father and the Savior of Our Country." At the right is his last photograph, showing the toll the Presidency took after the portrait at the beginning of this portfolio was drawn.

CHAPTER 23

ROAD TO VICTORY

The military aspect of the Civil War has always attracted the most attention. The roar of gunfire, the massed movements of uniformed men, the shrill of bugles, and the drama of hand-to-hand combat have fascinated students of warfare for a century. Behind the lines, however, life was less spectacular. It was the story of backbreaking labor to provide the fighting men with food and arms, of nerve-tingling uncertainty about the course of national events, of heartbreak over sons or brothers or husbands lost in battle. If the men on the firing lines won the victories, the means to those victories were forged on the home front.

Never in the nation's history had Americans worked harder for victory than in the Civil War. Northerners and Southerners alike threw themselves into the task of supplying their respective armies. Both governments made tremendous demands upon civil-

Robert E. Lee, commander of the Army of Northern Virginia for the major part of the war, was a brilliant military strategist. He, almost by himself, was responsible for the South's many victories against the Union's greater forces and supplies.

ians and, in general, received willing cooperation.

By 1863, the Northern war economy was rumbling along in high gear. Everything from steamboats to shovels was needed—and produced. Denied Southern cotton, textile mills turned to wool for blankets and uniforms. Hides by the hundreds of thousands were turned into shoes and harness and saddles; ironworks manufactured locomotives, ordnance, armor plate. Where private enterprise lagged, the government set up its own factories or arsenals. Agriculture boomed, with machinery doing the job of farm workers drawn into the army. King Wheat replaced King Cotton in the lexicon of foreign trade.

In short, everything that a nation needed to fight a modern war was produced in uncounted numbers. Inevitably there were profiteers with gold-headed canes and flamboyant diamond stickpins, but for every crooked tycoon there were thousands of ordinary citizens living on fixed incomes who did their best to cope with rising prices and still make a contribution to the war effort. Those who could bought financier Jay Cooke's war bonds; others knitted, sewed, nursed, or lent any other assistance in their power.

Life behind the Confederate lines was grimmer. At the outbreak of the war, the South was pitifully short of everything but good fighting men, and its economy moved backward at an accelerating pace as the conflict went on. Confederate currency, unbacked by a gold reserve, became worth less and less, until by the end of 1864 it was worth nothing at all. Although the South managed to keep its fighting men in weapons for four years (with a good part of those weapons captured from federal troops), it was hard-pressed to feed and clothe them. During the war, the Confederacy produced not a single mile of railroad track,

The South's main source of income, cotton, was often captured and sold to England by Northerners, as cartooned above. Another problem was her currency (below), which was never declared legal tender. Patriotism alone gave it value.

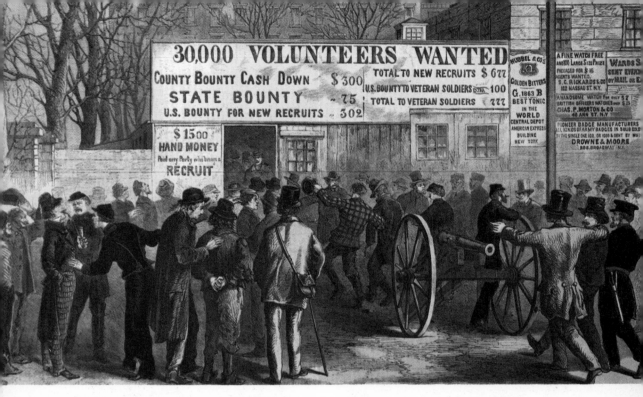

A recruiting scene in the North shows that the main appeal of the federal government was not to the patriotism of its men, but to their pocketbook.

and its antiquated transportation system was wholly incapable of the load it was asked to bear.

Southern citizens demonstrated the meaning of "total war" long before the term came into popular use. Few armies in world history have had more support and loyalty from the populace than those of the Confederate states. Southerners put their beliefs on the line, and gave until there was no more to give.

Finding soldiers to man the firing lines became increasingly difficult as the war dragged on. At first, volunteers made up the armies of both sides, but men who choose to go to war usually turn up where the fighting is heaviest. As a result, the ranks of the volunteers were soon decimated,

and both North and South turned to a military draft. The Confederacy's draft laws were reasonably fair, and on the whole its system was successful. But in the North the system was an atrocity. A man could pay to avoid the draft, or he could hire a substitute to go to war in his place. These substitutes were often the dregs of society, of no use whatever to the army.

The bounty system was another attempt to meet this problem. A sizable cash payment was offered to enlist (and, incidentally, avoid the draft). All that this proved, however, was that men who joined the army for money were seldom inclined to risk their lives. The system also produced a large number of bounty jumpers—men who accepted their bounty, de-

In Richmond's Libby Prison, over 1,000 Union officers were confined in eight rooms, like the one in David Blythe's painting, in an old tobacco warehouse.

serted at the first opportunity, rejoined for another bounty at another location, and repeated the whole process as long as they could evade detection.

Perhaps nothing more quickly dispels the romantic gloss sometimes applied to the Civil War than the story of the prisoner-of-war camps. These deathtraps lay like festering sores across the land, both North and South. In places such as Andersonville in Georgia, Libby Prison in Richmond, Camp Douglas near Chicago, and Elmira Prison in New York, men died like flies from untreated wounds, from starvation, and from any number of diseases. The statistics are appalling: Of the 350,000 men captured, nearly 50,000 died, and uncounted thousands suffered crippling ailments from which they never fully recovered. This was seldom the result of any conscious policy of brutality; prisoners simply succumbed to neglect, to bureaucratic inefficiency, to the heartlessness of war.

The industrial boom, the profiteers, the bounty jumpers, the prison camps, the sacrifices of the people at home—they were all threads of the fabric of a society torn by a civil war and changed forever. And no portion of that society was more radically changed than the "peculiar institution" of slavery. By 1863, the institution was visibly crumbling, thanks to the federal armies. General Sherman, returning from a raid in Mississippi, reported, "We bring in some 500 prisoners, a good many refugees, and about 10 miles of Negroes."

Many Northern soldiers had enlisted both to save the Union and destroy slavery. Others thought of the Union alone and cared little for the Negro. But all obeyed army orders, and if it was army policy to strip Southern plantations of their labor supply, they had little choice but to go along. The destruction of slavery was nowhere more evident than in the Mississippi Valley in 1863; then it became plain in the Eastern theater in 1864 as the Union Army began to penetrate deeply into the Confederacy.

Forcing the gateway

The armies of Lee and Meade in the East were exhausted after Gettysburg, and for the rest of 1863 they sparred and probed at each other to little effect. In addition, both generals had to feed men into the rapidly expanding cockpit of war in eastern Tennessee.

Even as Grant closed the ring on Vicksburg, and Lee marched to his fateful clash at Gettysburg, Rosecrans was pushing southward with the

Closing in on Chattanooga, the federal forces crossed the Tennessee River near Stevenson, Alabama. General Rosecrans is at the left, waving his sword.

671

William S. Rosecrans   *George H. Thomas*   *Braxton Bragg*

Army of the Cumberland. His goal was Chattanooga, the logical railroad base for any thrust into the Deep South. After a skillful campaign of maneuver, Rosecrans forced Bragg's Confederate Army of Tennessee out of Chattanooga and occupied the city on September 9.

The bulk of the federal army, however, was wandering around in the mountainous country of northern Georgia, trying to come to grips with Bragg's force. On September 19, the two armies met in the gloomy woodlands around Chickamauga Creek, a dozen miles south of Chattanooga. The fighting on the 19th was indecisive, but the next day James Longstreet—who had been sent west with two divisions from Lee's army— punched a hole in the Union center and split Rosecrans' army in half. Most of the routed Federals and their commanding officer fled toward Chat-

tanooga, but Major General George H. Thomas pulled enough men together to stand off the heavy Southern assaults. On that day Thomas earned a nickname, the Rock of Chickamauga, and bought enough time for the rest of the army to escape.

Chickamauga was the only important victory the Confederacy ever won in the Western theater—and Bragg proceeded to throw it away. Despite the pleadings of his officers, he let Rosecrans establish himself solidly in Chattanooga. The Southerner was content to occupy Missionary Ridge, overlooking the city, and try to starve the Federals into surrender.

The high command in Washington was spurred into action. Heavy reinforcements were dispatched from Meade's army in Virginia and Sherman's force in Memphis. Rosecrans was replaced by Thomas, and Grant

The Union and rebel forces met at Chickamauga on September 20, 1863. They were painted by William Travis as if locked in a fierce hand-to-hand combat.

was made supreme commander in the Western theater.

The first task was to open a supply line to beleaguered Chattanooga, which Grant and Thomas started to do. Now that they could again "board at home," as President Lincoln wrote, the Federals should attempt to break Bragg's siege lines. On November 25, 1863, this was done, by the soldiers of the Army of the Cumberland operating wholly on their own. These men had been humiliated by their defeat at Chickamauga and mercilessly derided by the reinforcements sent to "rescue" them, and they were fighting mad. They delivered, on orders, a feint at Missionary Ridge; then, without orders, they charged directly up the steep face of the ridge and sent Bragg's Confederates reeling into Georgia.

The fight at Missionary Ridge had momentous results. The North now had a springboard from which to launch a thrust into the heart of the Confederacy. William T. Sherman, newly appointed to command the Western theater, would lead this thrust. Most important, U. S. Grant was brought to Washington and named general-in-chief of all the Union armies. At last, after two and a half years of fighting, the federal war machine was to be directed by a soldier who knew exactly what he wanted to do and how to do it. This stocky, quiet man who looked, a fellow officer said, "as if he had determined to drive his head through a brick wall, and was about to do it" now began to forge a strategy that was to win the war for the North.

The Union offensive

As Grant saw it, the problem was deceptively simple. The Confederacy had two main armies—Lee's Army of

Hooker's capture of Lookout Mountain was more dramatic than decisive, and Grant re-

garded it simply as a first step in his general assault on Bragg's main Missionary Ridge line.

Northern Virginia encamped below the Rapidan River in Virginia, and the Army of Tennessee, now commanded by General Joseph E. Johnston (Bragg finally having been relieved), lying in north Georgia. The Confederate States of America could exist only as long as these two armies existed. Johnston was Sherman's assignment; Grant himself would travel with the Army of the Potomac against Lee. In May, 1864, the Federals began to move south.

Grant crossed the Rapidan and tried to march quickly through the Wilderness to turn Lee's flank. But the wily Confederate once more chose to make the Wilderness his battlefield. There ensued a desperate struggle in the tangled underbrush, with the acrid battle smoke hanging low under the treetops. It was, a Union soldier wrote, "simply bushwhacking on a grand scale." When the musketry sputtered out on May 6 after two days of fighting, Lee had won another victory, smashing in both ends of the federal line and inflicting 17,500 casualties at a cost of 8,000.

Grant shrugged off the defeat and pushed on southward. Lee managed to block his path at Spotsylvania

William Mahone's Confederate forces counterattack at Petersburg after the North had made several attempts to break through the Confederate defenses, but hard-fighting Mahone could do no more than re-establish his position.

676

Court House, and for 12 days the two armies slashed at each other.

On one of those days, May 12, the fighting reached a new pitch of intensity. Grant launched a powerful punch at the Confederate center, broke through, and then was held by counterattacks. For 18 solid hours, in a pelting rain, men in blue and gray killed one another at point-blank range at a spot in the Southern line known simply as Bloody Angle.

Grant finally broke off the action at Spotsylvania and continued his flanking operation. Once more the two armies conducted a nightmare race, aiming for the strategically important crossroads hamlet of Cold Harbor, east of Richmond. Grant again attempted a frontal attack and again failed, losing 7,000 men in 30 minutes. A Southern officer observed that the dead "covered more than five acres of ground about as thickly as they could be laid."

In a month of steady fighting, Grant's losses averaged 2,000 men a day, and anguished Northerners began calling him The Butcher. But that stubborn warrior, with grim logic, knew he could make his losses good while Lee could not.

Grant now changed his tactics and made a swift skillful flanking march past Richmond and across the James. His target was Petersburg, 20 miles

Ulysses S. Grant, photographed at City Point, Virginia, during the siege of Petersburg, was then a lieutenant general.

The Confederacy surrounded the city of Atlanta with strong lines of fortifications, even stripping the frame houses of their lumber to build trenches.

south of Richmond, through which passed nearly all the railroad lines that supplied both the Confederate capital and Lee's army.

The advance elements of the Army of the Potomac arrived before Petersburg on June 15. For once in his career, Robert E. Lee had been fooled, and his army was a day's march away. With a golden chance staring him in the face, the officer in charge of the Union spearhead bungled his attack on the thinly manned Petersburg fortifications. Then Lee's veterans arrived, and the chance was gone. The Federals settled down to lay siege.

Meanwhile, in Georgia, Sherman was fighting a different kind of war. He and Johnston moved crabwise across the northern half of the state,

William Tecumseh Sherman

Sherman, after taking Atlanta, went on his famous March to the Sea, burning houses and tearing up the railway lines he crossed.

thrusting, parrying, seeking an opening. On June 27, Sherman tried a frontal attack on the Confederates at Kennesaw Mountain and was beaten back with severe losses. He resumed his flanking operations. By mid-July, Johnston's outnumbered army was in the fortifications of Atlanta, a key manufacturing and transportation center. Sherman prepared for a siege.

Grant's strategy had succeeded in pinning down the two Confederate armies, but this fact was not quite clear to war-weary Northerners. All they could see was that no great victories had been won, and that the casualty lists were reaching proportions undreamed of in those far-off days of 1861. Abraham Lincoln was facing reelection in November, and he began

to feel he could not win. If he should lose, a negotiated peace would almost surely follow, with the South becoming an independent nation.

Closing the ring

Some people in the South—including General Johnston—saw quite clearly the problem Lincoln faced. To Johnston it seemed unlikely that the Confederacy could any longer win independence by military means; he felt that the only hope was to prolong the war until the North became tired of the death and destruction, repudiated Lincoln, and sued for peace. Jefferson Davis, however, saw things differently. To Davis, a military man himself, only military victories counted. In his view, Johnston had failed to fight. On July 17, 1864, he replaced Johnston with General John Bell Hood.

Hood was an impetuous Texan whose specialty was hard, head-to-head fighting. He had commanded superb assault troops under Lee, and had lost the use of an arm at Gettysburg and a leg at Chickamauga. As Sherman pressed his 100,000-man force on Atlanta, Hood went over to the attack.

On July 20, he hit the Federals as they crossed Peachtree Creek north of the city, but he was up against George Thomas, and Thomas threw him back. Hood tried again two days later in what was called the Battle of Atlanta. Once more he was stopped. On July 28, Hood launched a third assault, west of Atlanta at Ezra Church, only

COOK COLLECTION, VALENTINE MUSEUM

Jubal A. Early

Early made a surprise attack on Sheridan on October 19, 1864, just 20 miles south of Winchester, Virginia, and until Sheridan rallied his panic-stricken men (right), they were frantically retreating.

to be driven back with heavy losses. The city was now ringed on three sides, and the Confederate forces had to get out or be trapped. On September 2, Atlanta was occupied by federal troops. The Lincoln administration could at last announce a major victory.

At Petersburg, in that summer of 1864, a war of attrition was under way. Lee's entrenchments were too strong to break with frontal assaults, and Grant had to be content to use his superior manpower to extend his lines gradually, stretching the already thin gray ranks. It was pointed out to

Grant that the campaign resembled the Kilkenny cats that devoured each other. He admitted there was some truth to this, but added, "Our cat has the longer tail."

In desperation, Lee once more tried the tactic of threatening Washington. He sent hard-bitten Jubal A. Early and a small striking force north into the Shenandoah Valley. In July, Early tried a quick thrust at Washington, but he was blocked by the army corps that Grant quickly dispatched to the capital. As Early withdrew, Grant determined to take the Shenandoah Valley out of the war for good. This would not only close off Lee's favorite invasion route, but it would also eliminate a major source of food and forage for the Confederate forces. The job was given to a bandy-legged, hard-as-nails cavalryman named Philip Sheridan.

In September, Sheridan, pushing Early's outnumbered force before him, began to lay waste to the valley. Barns and corncribs and mills went up in smoke, livestock was slaughtered or driven away, and whole families—many of them pro-Union—were forced to evacuate their homes. This was total war. On October 19, Early auda-

681

April 9, 1865, Lee surrendered his army to Grant at Appomatox Court House.. The broadside below appeared in Detroit, expressing the joy of peace at last.

SURRENDER OF GEN. LEE!

"The Year of Jubilee has come! Let all the People Rejoice!"

200 GUNS WILL BE FIRED

On the Campus Martius,

AT 3 O'CLOCK TO-DAY, APRIL 10,

To Celebrate the Victories of our Armies.

Every Man, Woman and Child is hereby ordered to be on hand prepared to **Sing and Rejoice.** The crowd are expected to join in singing Patriotic Songs.

ALL PLACES OF BUSINESS MUST BE CLOSED AT 2 O'CLOCK.

Hurrah for Grant and his noble Army.

By Order of the People.

ciously attacked Sheridan's army at Cedar Creek, but with Sheridan himself rallying the surprised Federals, the Confederates were completely shattered and driven for good from the Shenandoah Valley.

The Democrats had nominated General George McClellan to oppose the President in the election. But between McClellan's nomination in August and the election in November, Sherman and Sheridan had dramatically put the federal war machine on the road to victory. The President was overwhelmingly re-elected. "I earnestly believe that the consequences of this day's work," Lincoln said, "will be to the lasting advantage, if not to the very salvation, of the country."

Triumph and tragedy

In Georgia in November there occurred one of the strangest scenes of the Civil War. Sherman and Hood turned their backs on each other and marched off in different directions. Hood gambled on one throw of the dice, driving north into Tennessee and hoping Sherman would follow. Sherman was delighted. "If he will go to the Ohio River, I'll give him rations,"

Grant's dispatch—"General Lee surrendered the Army of Northern Virginia this afternoon on terms proposed by myself"—brought the North scenes like this.

he announced. The Union general sent reinforcements to General Thomas at Nashville, burned a sizable part of Atlanta, and set about taking the State of Georgia out of the war.

Sherman's army, virtually unopposed, slashed a 60-mile-wide path of devastation from Atlanta to the sea. His men lived high off the land, burning or destroying what they could not eat or carry away. On the fringes of the army, deserters and riffraff known as bummers looted and burned dwellings as well. The March to the Sea was a grim lesson to the Confederacy that it could no longer defend its heartland, and it left an unhealing wound on the South. On December 22, Sherman seized Savannah and a great hoard of military supplies. He whimsically wired Lincoln, offering the city as a Christmas present.

Meanwhile, Hood's Army of Tennessee was on its last march. On November 30, at Franklin, Tennessee, the Confederates made a frontal attack not unlike Pickett's charge at Gettysburg. They were slaughtered. Undaunted, Hood moved on to Nashville. There, on November 15 and 16, George Thomas completely shattered the rebel army. The war in the West was over.

As 1864 became 1865, the Confederacy writhed in its death throes. Fort Fisher, guarding Wilmington, North Carolina, was captured by the Federals, closing the South's last door to the outside world. Sherman invaded South Carolina, burning and destroying as he went, and by March he was in North Carolina. In reality, the Confederacy existed now only in the person of Robert E. Lee and his beleaguered army at Petersburg.

In the first days of April, Grant broke through the Southerner's defenses. Lee evacuated Petersburg and Richmond and tried to get his army away to the West. Scenting victory, the long-suffering Army of the Potomac pursued vigorously. On April 9, at Appomattox Court House, Lee surrendered his starving and exhausted troops to Grant.

The Civil War had lasted almost exactly four years. It had cost over 600,000 lives (more than all of the nation's other wars combined), and wreaked incalculable damage on the land. But there remained one more scene to be acted out before the curtain came down on the American tragedy.

Abraham Lincoln had a vision of America, and he had stood in the center of the caldron of war to defend that vision. Somehow he forged the diverse and conflicting elements in the North into a force that in the end was triumphant. Then, on the night of April 14, 1865, at Ford's Theatre in Washington, an insane actor named John Wilkes Booth, professing allegiance to the Southern cause that he lacked the courage to fight for, mortally wounded the President. Lincoln died the next morning, and Secretary of War Edwin Stanton intoned, "Now he belongs to the ages."

MARINERS MUSEUM

THE NAVAL WAR

The battles on sea and river were an important part of the Civil War. First and foremost, they affected the South's economy and war materials. At the start of the conflict, the North began a blockade of the South's ports, keeping her cotton from going out and foreign military supplies from coming in. The North's eventual success in this effort was one of the main reasons for her victory, as it weakened the South economically and curtailed her ability to wage war. The battles were also a deciding factor in the action along the Mississippi River. They cut into the South's supply lines and damaged her deepest positions of strength, the loss of which often affected the pride that was so much a part of her reason for fighting. Finally, the naval war had meaning for the future of America. In both the North and the South, inventors applied their imagination to creating new forms of ship warfare. Ironclads, submarines, and torpedoes were put into use. The lack of metals and machinery in the South limited the scope of her inventions, but in the end they, too, became a part of the greater might of the united nation that was to come.

THE MAKESHIFT NAVY

St. George, Bermuda, enjoyed a wartime boom as a result of the Union blockade of the South. Here and in Nassau, cargoes from Europe were transferred from the ocean-going vessels to trimmer and faster blockade-runners for the final dash to the rebel ports.

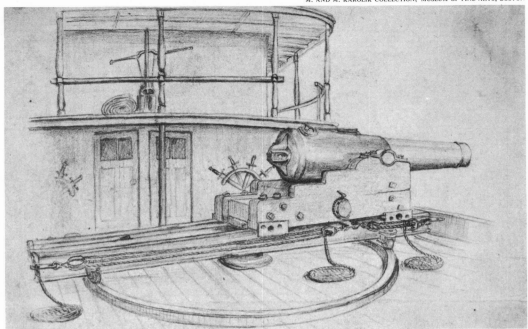

The above Mississippi River side-wheeler was first sunk by the Union Navy, then raised by it and made into a gunboat.

In 1861, Alex Simplot sketched the metamorphosis of the ferryboat *New Era* from a pleasure craft into a light-draft gunboat.

THE NAVAL WAR

THE NEW NAVY

Swedish immigrant John Ericsson designed the Union ironclad *Monitor* that was launched January 30, 1862, on the very same day as the *Merrimac*.

On March 8, the *Merrimac,* the South's ironclad, encountered Union ships, sinking the *Cumberland* and burning the *Congress.* On the next day, she (above, center) met the *Monitor* at Hampton Roads, where from eight in the morning until noon the ships battled, sometimes even touching each other, until the *Merrimac* retired, with the *Monitor* undamaged.

Commanded by Henry Walke, the federal gunboat *Carondelet* (above) was one of the eight ironclads James B. Eads built in St. Louis in 100 days with 4,000 men.

Below is Alex Simplot's painting of the brief, savage naval battle at Memphis. Of eight lightly armed and armored Confederate ships, only one escaped.

THE NAVAL WAR

INVENTIONS

There had been earlier attempts at designing a submarine, but it was not until Horace L. Hunley brought his frail, cigar-shaped iron boiler on a flatcar to Charleston in the summer of 1863 that the idea became a reality in war. There were many unsuccessful trials—20 men were killed, including Hunley—before a submarine, the *Hunley* (above), was launched on February 17, 1864. She sank a Union ship, but she and her crew also went down.

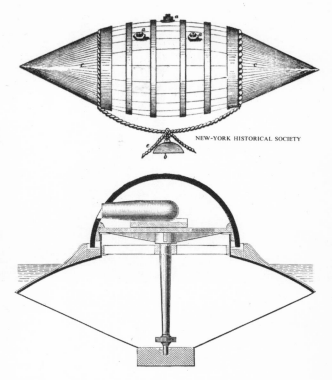

At the top is a Confederate mine that was made from a converted beer keg, and, under it, is John Ericsson's design for an armored turret. A Union impression of the *Hunley,* with the crew too large, is shown opposite. Below is the Dahlgren gun, with curved walls meant to keep it from exploding.

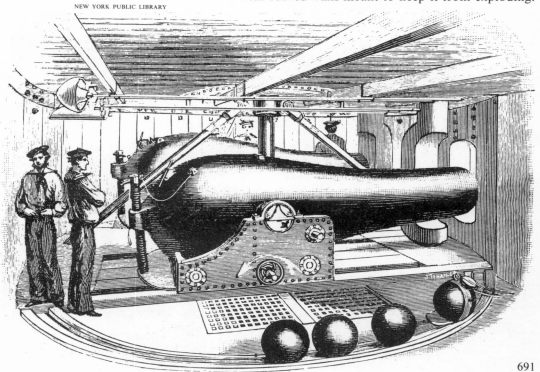

691

THE NAVAL WAR

BATTLES

Island No. 10, a Confederate fort on the Kentucky-Tennessee border of the Mississippi, surrendered to the Union Navy on April 7, 1862, after a month's bombardment by ironclads (left) and mortar boats.

At Vicksburg, Mississippi (below), Admiral David Porter's fleet ran past the city's guns on the night of April 16, 1863. On July 4, 1863, General Grant, moving in from the south, captured the city.

In one of the major battles of the war, the U.S.S. *Kearsarge,* under the command of Captain John A. Winslow, sank the rebel raider *Alabama* near Cherbourg, France, where she had gone for repairs.

OVERLEAF: On the morning of August 5, 1864, Admiral David Farrugut moved into Mobile Bay, his flagship *Hartford* deluged by gunfire, but by 10 o'clock that same morning he had taken the port.

CHAPTER 24

RECONSTRUCTION

On May 23 and 24, 1865, Americans and representatives from foreign lands crowded along Washington's Pennsylvania Avenue to watch the Grand Review. On the first day, General George Meade led the neat, seemingly endless ranks of the veteran Army of the Potomac on parade, before the admiring eyes of the excited crowds. Then, on the following day, Sherman's rough and ready Westerners, fresh from their history-making march through a shattered South, slouched along the avenue behind their grizzled leader. Washington was solidly decked with colored bunting and aflutter with thousands of flags. The holiday spirit was everywhere apparent. A scattering of empty sleeves and an occasional peg leg were about all that reminded the people of the grim past. The war was over, and to them the future was bright.

All across Dixie silence hung like a death pall. Soldiers came home quietly, grimly, to a tearful welcome. Their farms, their homes, their former

One of the themes of the United States centennial, as shown on this allegorical sheet-music cover, was the solidarity of the Union.

places of business frequently lay in ruins. Members of their families were often missing. The land and the people were exhausted from the protracted struggle.

Ahead lay an uncertain future. What would be the penalty for losing, and what sort of existence would the days ahead provide? These were the big questions. The South would be rebuilt, would live again and grow again. But under what conditions? Tight-lipped, Southerners waited to find out. All eyes were fixed upon Washington, upon Congress, and upon the new President from Tennessee, Andrew Johnson.

Americans discovered, in the years immediately following 1865, that the problems of peace were more complex than those of war. In the military conflict, violent and bloody as it had been, the road ahead was often well marked. The problems of peace were more subtle, more complex, more disturbing. They called for judgment, fairness, and thoughtful consideration, at a time when wartime passions still ran high. In 1865, hatreds smoldered, memories of personal losses were burned deeply into men's minds, and peace without revenge was hard to envisage.

The first postwar decade is usually referred to as the reconstruction era. Like so many terms, it does not correctly or completely describe or explain. It was not possible, in 1865, simply to reconstruct the United States as it had existed in 1861. The states were reassembled and called united, but the result was more than a repair job. It was a new nation.

Certainly the Old South was no more. Its labor base, slavery, was demolished and the day of the great plantation was gone. This did not mean that growing cotton would stop nor that the Negro would not grow it. But the plantation ideal—the Bourbon aristocrat at the top and slave labor at work in the fields—was a thing of the past. Cotton now would be grown by both white and colored men as sharecroppers, and a system of tenancy would replace the old slavery.

Like the South, the North could not be reconstructed to resemble its former self. Men of 1861 returned from the war fronts in 1865 to a newly industrialized and much more centralized country. Wartime demands for efficiency produced an era of expansion and consolidation that would continue throughout the century. The steel age was at hand, with its huge factories and its enormous productive capacity. The Homestead Act of 1862, coupled with wartime requirements for food, had revolutionized agricul-

ture. Farmers, blessed by high prices and presented with government lands, spent their money freely for farm machinery. In a single spurt, in just a few years, the North shot decades ahead of the South in agricultural development.

Moreover, there could be no reconstruction from a political standpoint. For the time being—indeed, until the election of Woodrow Wilson in 1912 —the United States was virtually a one-party nation. The only Democratic President between Buchanan and Wilson was Grover Cleveland. Except for Cleveland's two-term interruption, the Republicans had things pretty much their own way. It would take the Democratic Party more than a generation to recover its former strength.

Even those who ran the federal government could not agree upon the meaning of reconstruction. Lincoln believed it meant readjusting and realigning the Southern states to put them back into the Union. At no time did the President ever recognize the validity of secession. He took the view that these states had never left the Union, that they were, in a sense, merely "kidnapped" by individuals in arms against the government.

A number of Congressmen, including many members of Lincoln's own Republican Party, did not agree with him. They felt that it was impossible to "put Humpty Dumpty together again." These hardheaded Radical Republicans held that the Southern

Peace had been signed in April, 1865, and the troops had begun to return home, but on May 23 and 24, seemingly endless columns of men marched down Washington's Pennsylvania Avenue as the Union Army paraded in its final review.

"erring sisters" had left home for good and therefore had lost all former rights and privileges. To a large block of Republicans, the South was merely a conquered province, to be treated as one of the spoils of war.

The American people, as a whole, were eager for some kind of settlement. The majority looked forward to no more than the return of peace and "the good old days." In the North, there was a strong desire to reduce the large army and thereby weaken the power of the military regime that had controlled the country during the war. Civil justice had suffered in this period, and that fact went against the Anglo-Saxon tradition. Northerners also wanted to lower taxes as quickly as possible. In all these things, they anticipated a return to what they had known before. But this is something no postwar generation has ever been able to find.

Presidential reconstruction

Despite the wish to recapture peace and prosperity, the question of how to treat the conquered South remained the burning issue. Long before the war ended, there was talk about how the vanquished should be treated when the final gun had been fired. It was discussed as early as 1862. In December,

699

1863, Lincoln proposed that when one-tenth of the qualified Southern voters for the year 1860 took an oath of loyalty to the Constitution, they might set up a state government and ask for recognition by the federal government. This so-called One-Tenth Plan or Lincoln Plan (also referred to as the Louisiana Plan) assumed that at all times there had remained some loyal people in the South—people who never had lost their rights as Americans. Through the use of his Presidential power of pardon, Lincoln proposed to restore their full rights to them. Those who were sorry could say

so and would then be invited to return to the fold.

Lincoln's plan, announced at the height of the war, revealed his desire to show the world that the rebellion was coming to an end. A gradual re-entrance of states into the Union would be strong proof. In 1864, Louisiana and Arkansas and, in 1865, Tennessee held conventions and established loyal governments under the new plan. The furious Radicals in Congress were convinced that this meant a soft peace.

When Lincoln was assassinated, those who had opposed his plans for

This mowing machine was one of the many new inventions in the mid-19th century that was turning America into a land of agricultural and industrial wealth.

the South took new hope. The man whose credo was "With malice toward none; with charity for all" was dead, and in his place was Andrew Johnson, a Tennessee Unionist who had taken a pronounced stand against those in rebellion. Benjamin Wade, the militant Senator from Ohio, spoke for his Radical friends when he said, "Johnson, we have faith in you! By the gods, there will be no trouble now in running the government!"

Those who had hoped for a violently anti-Southern stand by Johnson were disappointed, however. His earlier sentiment that "treason is a crime and must be punished as a crime" was replaced by moderation and an almost complete acceptance of Lincoln's viewpoint.

Congress recessed soon after Johnson's accession to the Presidency. From April until December, when the next regular session convened, the members were at home. During their absence, Johnson took full advantage of the situation. Closely following Lincoln's earlier procedure, but making its stipulations slightly more strict, the new President reopened the doors of the Union. By December, 1865, all the seceded states but Texas had returned to the fold. When Congress met again, its members were amazed to find Southerners who had fought the Union only months before waiting to claim their seats.

Members of the Republican Party had more at stake than merely making a hard peace with the South. Before the war, under the provisions in Article I of the Constitution, only three-fifths of the Negro slave population was counted for Congressional representation. Now, with thousands of slaves at liberty, the Negro was no longer three-fifths of a man politically, but a whole man. This would mean at least 12 additional Southern Representatives in Congress. It is small wonder that the Radical Republicans were disturbed at the sudden return of the recalcitrant states. It meant they would have no opportunity to exercise any control over the South. It meant also that the Southerners were back, stronger than ever, in the halls of Congress. Republicans anxiously cast about for some way to deny them their seats.

Congressional reconstruction

An ancient rule came to the rescue of the Northern Congressmen, and through its application they took command of the reconstruction problem. Congress may pass upon the qualifications of its own members, excluding those who are deemed unfit to join the club. Radical Republicans seized upon this device to hold off the newly elected Southern members. It was a desperate move, one lacking in honesty and fairness, but those who invoked it were afraid that unless they took the initiative at that point, all would be lost.

The Radicals did not try to disqualify the Southerners permanently. They appointed a committee, made up

Benjamin F. Wade   Thaddeus Stevens   Edwin M. Stanton

Wade, Stevens, and Stanton were all members of the Radical wing of the Republican Party, which after the Civil War refused to accept the moderate measures for the reconstruction of the South that were instituted by Lincoln before his death and in part continued by his successor, Andrew Johnson.

of six Senators and nine Representatives, to study the matter. The delay would allow time to strengthen Republican Party lines and to make plans. Yet the move was more than a mere stalling measure. Led by vindictive Thaddeus Stevens of Pennsylvania, the group constituted a permanent committee on reconstruction. It spearheaded the Radical group in the Senate, whose members wanted sole control of the problem. The Committee of Fifteen, as it became known, was in no hurry. For six months it studied the whole question of reconstruction, of suffrage in the South, and of the status of those Southerners recently elected to Congress. During this time the unhappy applicants sat outside and waited.

The creation of Stevens' committee touched off warfare between Congress and Andrew Johnson, for its very existence challenged acceptance of the Southern states. Hostilities broke out in earnest during February, 1866, when Congress passed, and Johnson vetoed, a bill extending the Freedmen's Bureau. This organization, created originally to take care of the many newly freed Negroes, was singled out by the Radicals as an instrument for firm control of the Negroes politically. Johnson vetoed the bill and there were not enough votes to override his veto.

Congress tried to attack the problem directly when in March it passed the Civil Rights Bill, the provisions of which not only anticipated the Fourteenth Amendment by declaring that Negroes were citizens, but threatened to punish those states that failed to recognize it. Johnson promptly exercised his veto, but this time it was overridden. In July, the Radicals passed another Freedmen's Bureau bill and then overrode Johnson's veto. With this show of strength they began to get confident.

Congress next turned its attention to the Fourteenth Amendment. Laws may be rescinded or modified rather easily, but the Constitution is harder to tamper with. Republicans were eager to secure rights for the Negroes forever—not so much for humanitarian as for political reasons. The Negro population would account for some 30 Representatives in Congress, and there was no reason, in Republican minds, that they should not be members of that party. Here was the heart of the matter of reconstruction, from a Congressional point of view. It was an extreme stand—one that some of the conservatives in the Republican Party found hard to swallow, but to party leaders it was necessary for survival.

In writing the Fourteenth Amendment, its authors firmly imbedded into its first section the aims of the Civil Rights Act to avoid any future question of constitutionality on that score. Next they tried to force Southern states to give the Negro voting rights by threatening to reduce their representation in Congress if all male adult citizens in those states were not enfranchised. As a further blow to the South, it was provided that, unless pardoned by Congress, no supporter of the Confederacy who had formerly held a federal or state position could

Andrew Johnson

now hold office. Finally, the Confederate debt was repudiated and former masters of slaves were denied any compensation for their losses through emancipation.

Thus the Radical Congressmen tried to guarantee their notions of reconstruction by grafting them to the Constitution. The Thirteenth Amendment, which had granted all Negroes the freedom earlier expressed in Lincoln's Emancipation Proclamation, was the beginning. The Fourteenth Amendment, which mentioned only voting rights for "male inhabitants," now was fortified by a Fifteenth Amendment, which specifically provided that no one should be denied the ballot because of "race, color, or previous condition of servitude." The Radicals were determined to leave no loopholes for uncooperative Southern whites to slip through. The Constitution was to be the big weapon against an unfriendly state executive.

Andrew Johnson fought back, using every weapon in his power. In 1866, during the mid-term election, he toured the nation, blasting at his opponents and recommending the election of those who agreed with his position. The attempt was an utter failure, and the vote of confidence given the Radicals in their victory at the polls spurred them on to more audacious acts.

In March, 1867, Congress enacted legislation dividing the South into five military districts, each commanded by a general. The officers were to enroll all males, colored and white, and administer an oath of allegiance, after which those qualified to vote would elect representatives to state constitutional conventions. Each of the states

had to accept the idea of Negro suffrage and must approve the Fourteenth Amendment. Naturally, there were cries of "Unconstitutional," but when asked for its judgment, the Supreme Court declined to give it. This first Reconstruction Act, passed March 2, 1867, and shored up by three supplemental acts, fastened the grip of Congress upon the conquered South.

War on Capitol Hill

By the spring of 1867, the hard core of Radical Republicans in Congress were in the saddle and completely confident. By then, Presidential vetoes were laughably low hurdles to them. As chief executive, sworn to uphold the law of the land, Johnson was obliged to carry out Congressional wishes. He did his best, appointing military commanders who in turn set into motion in each of their districts

the machinery of reconstruction. During the winter and spring of 1867–68, the newly elected Southern conventions labored and, except for Texas, they completed their tasks of constitution-making.

But this was not enough for the vindictive elements in Congress. Mere supremacy over Johnson was too little for men bent on ruining him. In March, 1867, on the same day the first reconstruction bill became law, Congress also passed the Tenure of Office Act. This was designed to prevent Johnson from discharging hostile appointees and replacing them with his own supporters. Johnson vetoed the bill, of course, and it was promptly passed over his veto. Undaunted, the President held that the law was unconstitutional and therefore void. The Supreme Court, at the lowest ebb in its history, maintained complete silence. Proceeding alone, Johnson ignored the Tenure of Office Act. His enemies could have asked for nothing better, and they decided to ambush him.

The Radicals wanted to do something never before or since accomplished in American history. They wanted to impeach and convict the President, sending him home in disgrace. The difficulties were great, for they had no real grounds upon which to try the accused. Then, in 1868, Johnson dismissed Secretary of War Stanton. The House of Representatives voted to impeach the President, using his alleged violation of the Tenure of Office Act as the basis of the charges. By March, the American people witnessed the spectacle of their President on trial for his political life.

After weeks of testimony and acrimonious debate, the Senate, acting as a court, voted upon the 11 charges against Johnson. None of the accusations, except perhaps violation of the Tenure of Office Act, had any substance, and even that one certainly did not approach anything resembling treason, bribery, or a high crime. There were 54 men in the Senate, and two-thirds had to vote against Johnson to convict him. If he could muster 19 votes, he was safe. He managed exactly that number on each of the charges. By a single vote the Radicals failed in their unprecedented attempt to destroy a political enemy. As it was, they made history, however unsavory. No Congress since has come close to

The great rush at the left is for the galleries of the Senate to hear Thaddeus Stevens deliver the impeachment message on February 25, 1868. The ticket is for Johnson's friends—and enemies—who wanted to see the impeachment proceedings.

matching the audacity of that move.

The very closeness of the impeachment-trial vote indicated the extent of the Republican power in Congress. A few days after Johnson's narrow escape, his enemies moved off to Chicago for the Republican national convention. There they nominated Ulysses S. Grant, hero of Appomattox and professional soldier, as their Presidential candidate. Schuyler Colfax, Speaker of the House and thoroughgoing Radical, was named as his running mate. It was regarded as an unbeatable team, a supposition that was wholly correct. Here were men who would work with the Radicals, men who would help insure the victory over the South and the permanency of the Grand Old Party.

Late in June, Congress again turned to the matter of the South. Back in 1866, Tennessee had been readmitted, and early in June, 1868, Arkansas was also. During that same month, North Carolina, South Carolina, Louisiana, Georgia, Alabama, and Florida were found to be pure enough for membership. Each of these states had to approve the Fourteenth Amendment. All of them except Georgia satisfactorily fulfilled their requirements, and by July they were again represented in Congress. In 1870, Mississippi, Texas, and Virginia returned. Now 10 of the 11 Confederate states were "reconstructed." Only Georgia remained outside the Union, still struggling with the strictures laid down by unbending Northerners in Congress. By 1871, she

was pronounced "tamed," and her Senators were at last seated.

Meanwhile, the Union's foremost war hero was elevated to the Presidency. Grant's election was a simple operation. His name was familiar in every household; when the grizzled, taciturn veteran said, "Let us have peace," the nation reacted favorably. Against such a powerful attraction, the Democratic candidate, Horatio Seymour, had little chance. He and his party were still tainted by their sympathies toward the South.

During Grant's first term, the nation was reconstructed in a narrow political sense. All the errant states resumed their former places, and each was represented in Congress. But there the comparison with prewar days ended. Northern "carpetbaggers" swarmed over the South, occupying key offices and controlling the political apparatus. They were aided by Southern "scalawags," another group of opportunists motivated by desires for personal gain.

With the Thirteenth, Fourteenth, and Fifteenth Amendments rammed down Southern throats, a large Negro population was enfranchised. The carpetbaggers, backed up by army bayonets, saw to it that these newcomers to suffrage voted the right way. Buying and selling votes became a common practice. Before long, the Southern political scene was one of chaos.

It is wholly understandable that Southerners reacted violently against the work of reconstruction architects in Washington. Under the carpetbag governments, state after state went bankrupt, corruption rose to heights that opened the eyes of the most hardened Americans, and the newly enfranchised Negro, along with his white sponsors, kept social relationships in an uproar. The Negro, a mere pawn in the game, became the object of Southern hatred, and it was upon him that retribution fell.

As early as 1866, an organization known as the Ku Klux Klan appeared in Tennessee. Its purpose was to control the Negro, and consequently his carpetbagger sponsors, through terrorism. Hooded and robed night riders paid calls upon the colored electorate, and by means of tricks and threats, frightened the ignorant and suspicious Negroes. When threats failed, violence was used. As with all such informal organizations, membership was not highly selective. The original intent of the Klan was largely forgotten, and beating, maiming, and murder were often used to settle personal disputes. This brought action from the government. In 1871, Congress passed severe anti-Klan legislation, and mass arrests followed. The measures were so effective that the Klan was almost eliminated that very year.

The progress of reconstruction was a source of increasingly strong complaint from Southerners. This only convinced many a vindictive Northerner that the correct medicine was being prescribed. While the South writhed in its agonies, the rest of the

PUCK WANTS "A STRONG MAN AT THE HEAD OF GOVERNMENT" --BUT NOT THIS KIND.

This cartoon indicates that Ulysses S. Grant was a strong President, but implies that all his strength went into supporting his corrupt followers in government positions. The two figures at the right are William W. Belknap, the Secretary of War, who was accused of taking bribes for the sale of trading posts in Indian territory; and O.E. Babcock, Grant's private secretary, who was indicted for defrauding the Internal Revenue department.

nation embarked upon a postwar boom, marred only by a slight recession in 1866. For the next decade, inflation and expansion were the economic bywords. Thriving industries worked to supply goods for a growing population and to catch up on the wartime lag in civilian production.

Grant was re-elected in 1872, despite a brief rebellion among Republican liberals. Some of the voters agreed that too much corruption accompanied the economic resurgence, and they voted for the Liberal Democrat, Horace Greeley, but in the main the electorate preferred to let the general have another term. It was hard for Northerners to vote against good times and a thoroughly subjugated South. For such benefits they could afford to put up with considerable corruption. Or so they imagined.

By 1876, times had changed. The war was more than a decade past and much of the Northern bitterness had subsided. Conditions in the South were such that many a Yankee was ready to relent and say that the vanquished had had enough. In the North, the financial panic of 1873 deeply disturbed the business world, causing a good deal of critical comment about government policies. During these times, corruption had surged so high in official circles that the Presidential family itself was touched.

Warning flags popped up in 1874, when in the mid-term election 23 states went Democratic. Two years later, as America's 100th birthday approached and centennial planners made ready to celebrate, voters became thoughtful. Was this the America that the Founding Fathers had envisaged? Was the theory of democracy working as well as they had hoped? Such questions must have caused thinking men to squirm as they looked at the state of public morals.

After failing for nearly 20 years to elect a candidate, the Democrats touched a sensitive political nerve by nominating a recognized reformer, Samuel J. Tilden, governor of New York. The Republicans chose Rutherford B. Hayes of Ohio, largely as a result of the battle between the Grant bitter-enders and the supporters of James G. Blaine. Hayes was a compromise candidate.

The Democrats proved that reform was a popular campaign issue when their candidate polled more popular votes than his opponent in the election. But those in office were determined to stay there, even if it resulted in a national scandal. Resolutely they set about upsetting the will of the electorate.

Seizing upon charges of fraud and violence in Louisiana, Florida, and South Carolina, Republican campaign managers challenged the election. They also questioned one of the electoral votes from Oregon. To squabble over a single vote might appear petty, but in this case it was vital. Tilden had 184 votes in the electoral college. Just one of the disputed votes would put him in office. The Republicans, on the other hand, had to have all of them.

The issue was decided by a commission of 15—five Senators, five Representatives, and five Supreme Court justices. That group divided, seven to seven, leaving in the hands of a single man the decision that would determine a President of the United States. Judge Joseph P. Bradley, a Republican, cast the deciding vote, and in all cases the answer was the same—eight to seven in favor of Hayes. It is small wonder that 19th-century "men of '76," especially the disappointed Democrats, may have thought in revolutionary terms. To them it appeared that the democratic process had failed, as indeed it had. At the time, many did not know that the outcome was determined by a deal whereby Southern Democratic leaders agreed to the Hayes victory, provided federal troops

The corruption of the carpetbaggers and Grant's violent bayonet rule of the South is attacked in this anti-Republican cartoon that was drawn around 1877.

were withdrawn from the South and at least one Southerner was appointed to the Cabinet. Such knowledge would have done little to strengthen the common man's belief in his political system.

Hayes realized the narrowness of his victory. He knew the temper of the opposition party, not to mention the frustration of the typical Southerner. The country at large was edgy and nervous, and the new President proceeded carefully. One of his first acts in office was to recall army units from the South. They provided the main support of carpetbag governments, and without them the whole false structure collapsed. This is precisely what the Southerners had foreseen, and it was why they had been willing to submit to the compromise that made Hayes President. With this single act, a new political power was created—the "solid South." For the remainder of the century, and well into the next, the Democratic Party was able to rely upon its unfailing support.

The immediate result of relaxing the military grip upon the South was, for all practical purposes, to end reconstruction. Emotional scars would remain for a long time and there would be a lingering bitterness, but once again Southerners had control of the political machinery, and they made the most of their situation.

In retrospect, it is clear that reconstruction was a many-sided failure. It failed politically in that Republican efforts to control the South, through the three amendments to the Constitution, did not produce the desired results. It was one thing to gain Negro suffrage by threat and force; it was something else to get the colored voter to the polls in the South. Local laws and terror tactics kept thousands away. The result was bitterness by Southern whites and a deep hatred for the Republican Party. Only bayonets could preserve Republican control, and that situation had to come to an end sometime in a country that stood before the world as a democracy.

Reconstruction was a social failure as well. Radical Republicans imagined they could legislate the Negro into a condition of equality, as if by waving a magic wand. There is no question that the former slave had every right to such a reward, but he was far from ready to receive it at that time. Worse, with Northern whites forcing the issue and Southern whites resisting it, the unfortunate Negro was ground between the upper and lower millstones of political power. When Southerners discriminated against the Negro, it was not only an attempt to control him, but at the same time to strike out at the freedman's Northern sponsors. Many a Negro, who long had enjoyed the care and affection of his white master and other whites, now became the subject of racial discrimination. And his torment came from no action of his own.

Attempts at economic reconstruction also failed for the Negro. In most

The lot of the Negro did not greatly improve after the war. He had to go back to raising cotton, this time as a hired field hand or a sharecropper.

cases he merely moved from slavery to a kind of peonage known as share-cropping. As a tenant farmer, he was dependent upon a landlord, and he found it almost as hard to escape from the new slavery as from the old. There was not much the Radicals could do about this situation, except confiscate Southern land and distribute it among Negroes. This was not done, although there was talk of it. In the early postwar period, many a Negro thought he was going to be awarded "40 acres and a mule," as he put it. When the "promised land" did not materialize, the Negro hired out as a field hand or became a share cropper, and went back to raising cotton. He had legal freedom, but neither economic nor social freedom.

Thus the postwar decade, often referred to as the reconstruction period, was a time of trial for the South and for the very forces of democracy itself across the country. The nation was not reconstructed or restored to what it had been. Instead, the war-torn South was held in a state of subjection as the North grew and prospered. In many ways, the political retribution that followed the war left deeper scars than those caused by shot or shell. The crop the Radicals sowed was hatred, and it grew well in the hothouse climate the Republican Party provided for it.

MAIN TEXT CONTINUES IN VOLUME 9

In Civil War slang, an "old soldier" was one who was able to devise ways to escape work or to avoid doing special duty. One of the many ways—some of which still exist in today's army—was to feign an illness that would put him in the hospital or on sick leave. Winslow Homer's painting entitled Playing Old Soldier shows a private who is, despite his unhappy face, not sick at all. Presumably the doctor and his orderly have seen enough of such malingerers to make and record a realistic diagnosis.

"Hayfoot, Strawfoot!"

A SPECIAL CONTRIBUTION BY
BRUCE CATTON

The Civil War soldier did what came naturally and usually lacked adequate military training. He was basically a civilian in arms and had much in common with today's G. I.

The volunteer soldier in the American Civil War used a clumsy muzzle-loading rifle, lived chiefly on salt pork and hardtack, and retained to the very end a loose-jointed, informal attitude toward the army. But despite the surface differences, he was blood brother to the G.I. Joe of modern days.

Which is to say that he was basically a civilian in arms. His attitude toward discipline, his officers, and the whole spit-and-polish concept of military existence was essentially one of careless tolerance.

What really set the Civil War soldier apart was the fact that he came from a less sophisticated society. The America of the 1860s was still essentially a rural nation; people lived largely on farms or in country towns and had a hayseed-in-the-hair flavor. For example, every war finds some ardent but underage youngsters who want to enlist. Such a lad today simply swears he is 18 and signs up. The lad of the 1860s felt that to lie to his own government was just plain wrong. So he would scribble the number 18 on a bit of paper and put it inside his shoe. Then, when the recruiting officer asked his age, he could look him straight in the eye and truthfully say, "I am over 18."

The drill sergeants repeatedly found that among the raw recruits there were men so abysmally untaught that they did not know left from right. To teach them how to march, the sergeants would tie a wisp of hay to the left foot and a wisp of straw to the right; then, giving the command to march, they would chant "Hayfoot, strawfoot! Hayfoot, strawfoot!" until everybody had caught on. A common name for a green recruit in those days was "strawfoot."

On the drill field, the men were likely to intone a little rhythmic chant—thus:

March! March! March, old soldier, march!
Hayfoot, strawfoot,
Belly full of bean soup—
March, old soldier, march!

Because of his unsophistication, the Civil War recruit usually joined up with romantic ideas about soldiering. He thought army life was going to be fun. And right at the start, it did have an almost idyllic quality. An Illinois recruit confessed, "It is fun to lie around, face unwashed, hair uncombed, shirt unbuttoned, and everything un-everthinged. It sure beats clerking." Another Illinois boy said, "I don't see why people will stay at home when they can get to soldiering. A year of it is worth getting shot for to any man." The chief worry, in training camp, was that the war would be over before the ardent young recruits could get into it. There was a regiment recruited in northern Pennsylvania in 1861—the 13th Pennsylvania Reserves, known as the Bucktails because the rookies decorated their caps with strips of deer hide. These youthful soldiers, ordered to rendezvous at Harrisburg, marched to the north branch of the Susquehanna, where they built rafts and floated down the river, singing, firing their muskets, and having a gay old time, camping out along the bank at night. Finally they got to Harrisburg, and they served through the worst of the war. They lost most of their men, but they never forgot those first days of army life, when they drifted down a river with a song in the air and the bright lights of adventure shining just ahead.

Discipline in those early regiments was pretty sketchy. Most of them were recruited locally, and everybody more or less knew everybody else. Therefore, the privates knew their officers—whom they usually had

As long as a man could and would fight, no one cared how he wore his cap or carried his rifle.

elected—so they never saw any need to be formal with them. Within reasonable limits, the Civil War private was willing to do what his company commander told him, but he saw little point in carrying it to extremes.

An Indiana soldier wrote, "We had enlisted to put down the Rebellion, and had no patience with the red-tape tomfoolery of the regular service. The boys recognized no superiors, except in the line of legitimate duty. Shoulder straps waived, a private was ready at the drop of a hat to thrash his commander— a thing that occurred more than once." A New York regiment, drilling on a hot parade ground, heard a private call to his company commander, "Say, Tom, let's quit this darn foolin' around and go over to the sutler's and get a drink." If an officer got complete obedience, he got it because the men recognized him as a natural leader and not because he had a commission.

The Civil War soldier's first loyalty was usually to his regiment, and odd rivalries developed. Outside Washington, a Manhattan regiment was camped near a regiment from Brooklyn. Neither had a chaplain, and one day a minister came to the Manhattan colonel and volunteered to hold religious services for his men. The colonel said his men were rather irreligious, not to say godless, and he feared they would not give the reverend a respectful hearing. The minister replied that he had just held services with the Brooklyn regiment, and the men there had seemed very devout. That was enough for the colonel. He ordered his men paraded for divine worship, and announced that anyone who talked, laughed, or even coughed would be court martialed.

So the clergyman held the services, and everyone was attentive. At the end of his sermon, the minister asked if any man wanted to make public profession of faith; in the Brooklyn regiment, he said, 14 men had. Instantly the New York colonel bellowed, "We're not going to let that Brooklyn regiment beat us at anything! Detail 20 men and have them baptized at once!"

The 48th New York was said to have an unusually large number of ministers serving

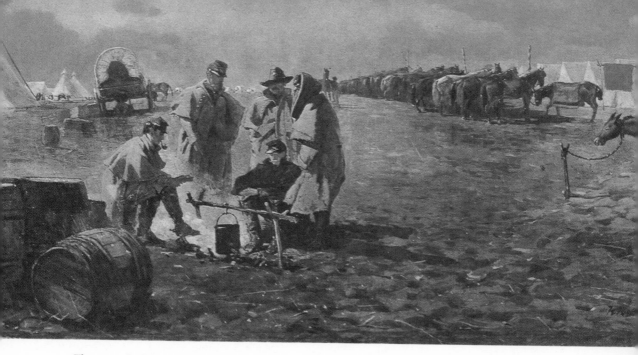

The group huddled around the fire in this Winslow Homer painting is probably preparing its own food. In the Civil War anyone became the cook who was assigned to the job.

as combat soldiers. The 48th, fairly early in the war, found itself posted in a South Carolina swamp, toiling in semitropical heat. All hands became excessively profane, including the onetime clergymen. A visiting general asked the regiment's lieutenant colonel if he himself was a minister in private life.

"Well, no, General," said the officer apologetically. "I can't say that I was a regularly ordained minister. I was just one of these —— —— local preachers."

Another story was hung on this same 48th New York. A Confederate ironclad gunboat was ready to steam through the swamp and attack the 48th's outposts, and elaborate plans were made to trap it. But it occurred to the colonel that the soldiers could not get into it; it was sheathed in iron, and all its ports would be closed. Remembering that many of his men had come from the less savory districts of New York City, he paraded the regiment and (according to legend) announced, "Now, men, you've been in this cursed swamp for two weeks—up to your ears in mud, no fun, no glory, and blessed poor pay. Here's a chance. Let every man who has had experience as a cracksman or a safeblower step to the front." To the last man, the regiment marched forward four paces and came to attention.

Not unlike this was the reputation of the 6th New York, which included so many Bowery toughs that the rest of the army said a man had to be able to show he had done time in prison in order to get in. The regiment was about to leave for the South, and the colonel gave his men an inspirational talk. They were going, he said, to a land of wealthy plantation owners, where each Southerner had riches of which he could be despoiled. He took out his own gold watch and held it up for all to see, remarking that any deserving soldier could easily get one like it, once he got down to plantation-land. Half an hour later, wanting to know the time, the colonel felt for his watch. It was gone.

If the Civil War army spun lighthearted tales about itself, it had to face a reality that was singularly unpleasant. One of the worst aspects had to do with food. From first to last, no men were enlisted as cooks. A company would simply be issued a quantity of provisions—flour, pork, beans, potatoes, and so on —and invited to prepare the stuff as best it could. Half a dozen men would form a mess and take turns cooking, and everybody had to eat what was prepared or go hungry. Later in the war, each company commander would usually detail two men to act as cooks, and if either knew anything about cooking, the company was in luck. One soldier asserted flatly, "A company cook generally knows less about cooking than any other man in the company. Not being able to learn the drill, and too dirty to appear on inspection, he is sent to the cook house to get him out of the ranks." When an army was on the march, the ration issue usually consisted of salt pork, hardtack, and coffee. The hardtack was good enough, if fresh, which was not always the case; with age it usually got infested with weevils, and veterans remarked that it was better to eat it in the dark.

In the Union Army, most of the time, the soldier could supplement his rations (if he had money) by buying extras from the sutler—a civilian merchant licensed to accompany the army, functioning somewhat as the post exchange does nowadays. The sutler charged high prices and specialized in indigestibles like pies and canned lobster, and those who patronized him regularly came down with stomach upsets. The Confederate Army had few sutlers, which helps to explain why the hungry Confederates were so delighted when they could capture a Yankee camp: To seize a sutler's tent meant high living for the captors, and the men in Lee's army were furious when, in the 1864 campaign, they learned Grant had ordered his army to move without sutlers.

If Civil War cooking arrangements were impromptu and imperfect, the same applied to its hospital system. The surgeons usually were good men by the standards of that day, but no one knew anything about germs or about how wounds became infected, and antisepsis in the operating room was unknown also. It is common to read of a surgeon whetting his scalpel on the sole of his shoe just before operating. The hospital attendants and stretcher-bearers

Food had to be found for the Civil War armies, and the means were often not those of peacetime. This wild group is raiding a farm, grabbing up everything that is in sight.

COLLECTION OF C. C. TRAVIS

716

were detailed from the ranks, and the officer usually chose his most worthless men. As a result, the sick or wounded often got atrocious care.

A result of all this—coupled with the fact that many men enlisted without any medical examinations—was that every regiment suffered a constant attrition from illness and disability. On paper, a regiment was supposed to have between 960 and 1,040 men. A veteran regiment that could muster 350 enlisted men present for duty was considered pretty solid. About twice as many Civil War soldiers died of disease—typhoid, dysentery, and pneumonia were the great killers—as died in action, and besides those who died, many more got medical discharges.

In its wisdom, the Union set up a number of base hospitals in Northern states, far from the battle fronts, on the theory that a man recovering from wounds or sickness would recuperate better back home. Unfortunately, these hospitals were under local control, and the men in them were no longer under the orders of their own regiments or armies. So thousands of men who were sent north for convalescence never returned to fight. Many were detailed for light work in the hospitals, and there they stayed because nobody had the authority to send them back to duty. Others, recovering their health, simply went home. They were answerable to the hospital authorities, not to the army command, and the hospital rarely cared much where they were. The whole system was ideally designed to make desertion easy.

Moreover, many men had little understanding of military discipline. A homesick boy often saw nothing wrong in going home to see the folks. A man from the farm might slip off to put in a crop. Both meant to return but would postpone it from week to week and perhaps end as deserters. This merely reflected the loose discipline and the underlying civilian-mindedness of the rank-and-file soldier. The behavior of Northern armies in Southern territory reflected the same thing—and had a profound effect on the institution of slavery.

Armies of occupation always bear down hard on civilian property. Northern armies

News from home was vital to these Southern soldiers, as it has always been to men at the front.

bore down with especial fervor. Chickens, hams, corn—anything edible that might be found on a plantation—looked like fair game. The typical Northern soldier had strong feelings about the evils of secession. To him the Southerners, being rebels, had forfeited their rights; if evil things happened to them, that was no more than just retribution.

William Tecumseh Sherman is thought of as the archetype of the Northern soldier who believed in pillage and looting, yet during the first years of the war, he resorted to ferocious punishments to keep his men from despoiling Southern property. He even had looters tied up by the thumbs, and all to little effect. Long before he started to commandeer or destroy property as a war measure, his soldiers were practicing it against his will. It was common for a Union colonel to point to a nearby farm and say, "Now, boys, that barn is full of nice fat pigs and chickens. I don't want to see any of you take any of them," whereupon he would look sternly in the opposite direction.

One colonel, punishing some men who had robbed a chicken house, said angrily, "Boys, I want you to understand that I am not punishing you for stealing but for getting caught at it."

Many a family saw the foodstuffs needed for the winter swept away in an hour by grinning hoodlums who could not use a quarter of what they took. Among the foragers there were many lawless characters who took watches and jewels; men would take a piano apart and use the wires to hang pots and pans over the campfire. The Civil War was romantic only at a considerable distance.

The Union soldiers also came to believe that to destroy Southern property was to help win the war. It is at this point that the institution of human slavery enters the picture.

Most Northern soldiers had little feeling against slavery, and little sympathy for the Negro himself. They were fighting to save the Union, not to end slavery. Nevertheless, they moved effectively to destroy slavery, because they were operating against Southern property and the most easily removable property was the slave. To help the slaves escape was to weaken Southern productive capacity, which in turn weakened Confederate armies. Hence the Union soldier took the "peculiar institution" apart, chattel by chattel, and thus weakened it fatally long before the war ended.

Chiefly, of course, the business of the Civil War soldier was to fight. He fought with weapons that look crude to modern eyes, and he moved by an outmoded system of tactics. The standard infantry weapon in the Civil War was the rifled Springfield—a muzzle-loader firing a conical lead bullet, usually of .54 caliber.

Loading was laborious, and only a good man got off more than two shots a minute. The weapon had a range of nearly a mile, and its "effective range"—that is, the range at which it would hit often enough to make infantry fire truly effective—was about 250 yards. Compared with a modern Garand, the old muzzle-loader is a museum piece; but compared with the weapons on which infantry tactics in the 1860s were based, it was fearfully destructive and efficient. The infantry still moved and fought in the formations of the days of smoothbore muskets, whose effective range was no more than 100 yards and which were wildly inaccurate at any distance.

Armies using those weapons attacked in solid mass formations, the men standing elbow to elbow. They could quickly get from effective range to hand-to-hand fighting, and if they had the right numerical advantage over the defensive line, they could come to grips without losing too many men. But in the Civil War, men would be hit while the rival lines were still half a mile apart, and to advance in mass was to invite wholesale destruction. Tactics had not yet been adjusted to the new rifles; thus attacks could be fearfully costly. And when the defenders dug entrenchments and got some protection, as they fast learned to do, a direct frontal assault could be hardly more than mass suicide. It took the high command a long time to revise their tactics, and battles ran up dreadful casualty lists. For an army to lose 25% of its numbers in a major battle was not uncommon, and in some fights—the Confederate Army at Gettysburg is an outstanding example—the percentage of loss ran close to one-third. Individual units were sometimes nearly wiped out. Some of the Union and Confederate regiments that fought at Gettysburg lost up to 80% of their numbers.

The point is that the discipline that took the Civil War soldier into action, although it was sketchy by modern standards, was nevertheless highly effective in battle. Any armies that could go through such battles as Antietam, Stone's River, Franklin, or Chickamauga and come back for more had little to learn about the business of fighting.

Perhaps the Confederate General D. H. Hill said it once and for all. At the Battle of Malvern Hill, George B. McClellan's men fought a rear-guard action—a bitter, confused fight that came at the end of a solid week of wearing, costly battles and forced marches. Federal artillery wrecked the Confederate assault columns, and as Hill looked out over the battlefield, strewn with dead and wounded boys, he reflected upon the valor of the two armies. He never forgot this, and looking back on it, long after the war was over, he declared in substance, "Give me Confederate infantry and Yankee artillery and I'll whip the world!"

Bruce Catton, Senior Editor of American Heritage Magazine, *has won the Pulitzer Prize for* A Stillness at Appomatox *and is the author of several other Civil War books.*

FOR FURTHER READING

The American Heritage Picture History of the Civil War. New York: American Heritage, 1960. With a narrative by Bruce Catton and many contemporary paintings, drawings, and photographs, as well as specially prepared maps, this work is unique among Civil War histories.

Beale, Howard. *The Critical Year: A Study of Andrew Johnson and Reconstruction.* New York: Harcourt, Brace, 1930.

Bowers, Claude G. *The Tragic Era.* Boston: Houghton Mifflin, 1929. A popularized account of reconstruction.

Catton, Bruce. *Mr. Lincoln's Army.* Garden City: Doubleday, 1951. *Glory Road.* Garden City: Doubleday, 1952. *A Stillness at Appomattox.* Garden City: Doubleday, 1953. *This Hallowed Ground.* Garden City: Doubleday, 1956. Four books on the Civil War by its foremost scholar.

Donald, David. *Lincoln Reconsidered.* New York: Knopf, 1956. New views on Lincoln.

Freeman, Douglas Southall. *Lee's Lieutenants.* 3 volumes. New York: Scribner, 1942-44. One of the classic military studies of Southern strategy and tactics.

Henry, Robert Selph. *The Story of Reconstruction.* Indianapolis: Bobbs-Merrill, 1938.

Josephson, Matthew. *The Politicos, 1865-1896.* New York: Harcourt, Brace, 1938. Politics during the reconstruction period.

Lewis, Lloyd. *Captain Sam Grant.* Boston: Little, Brown, 1950. The first and only volume in a study of Grant that Lewis left incomplete at his death. *Sherman: Fighting Prophet.* New York: Harcourt, Brace, 1932. The best biography of Sherman.

Milton, George Fort. *The Age of Hate: Andrew Johnson and the Radicals.* New York: Coward-McCann, 1930. The difficulties that Johnson encountered after the Civil War.

Randall, James G. *The Civil War and the Reconstruction.* Revised by David Donald. Boston: Heath, 1961. A complete general history of the war.

Sandburg, Carl. *Abraham Lincoln: The War Years.* 4 volumes. New York: Harcourt, Brace, 1939. The most ambitious modern study of Lincoln as President.

Thomas, Benjamin Platt. *Abraham Lincoln.* New York: Knopf, 1952. The most satisfactory single-volume biography of Lincoln.

Williams, Kenneth. *Lincoln Finds a General: A Military History of the Civil War.* 4 volumes. New York: Macmillan, 1949-56. The campaigns in detail from the Northern point of view.

Williams, Thomas Harry. *Lincoln and the Radicals.* Madison: University of Wisconsin Press, 1941. The differences between Lincoln and the Radical elements of his party.

Wilson, Edmund. *Patriotic Gore: Studies in the Literature of the American Civil War.* New York: Oxford University Press, 1962. A brilliant study of various writers and figures of the Civil War that presents many new and perceptive insights into the nature of the struggle and the reasons for it.

Woodward, C. Vann. *Reunion and Reaction.* Boston: Little, Brown, 1951. An important work dealing with the conclusion of the reconstruction period.

THE AMERICAN HERITAGE NEW ILLUSTRATED HISTORY OF THE UNITED STATES

PUBLISHED BY DELL PUBLISHING CO., INC.

George T. Delacorte, Jr., *Publisher* Helen Meyer, *President*
William F. Callahan, Jr., *Executive Vice-President*

Walter B. J. Mitchell, Jr., *Project Director;* Ross Claiborne, *Editorial Consultant;* William O'Gorman, *Editorial Assistant;* John Van Zwienen, *Art Consultant;* Rosalie Barrow, *Production Manager*

CREATED AND DESIGNED BY THE EDITORS OF AMERICAN HERITAGE MAGAZINE

James Parton, *Publisher;* Joseph J. Thorndike, Jr., *Editorial Director;* Bruce Catton, *Senior Editor;*
Oliver Jensen, *Editor;* Richard M. Ketchum, *Editor, Book Division;* Irwin Glusker, *Art Director*

ROBERT R. ENDICOTT, *Project Editor-in-Chief*

James Kraft, *Assistant Editor;* Nina Page, Evelyn H. Register, Lynn Marett, *Editorial Assistants;*
Lina Mainiero, *Copy Editor;* Murray Belsky, *Art Director;* Eleanor A. Dye, *Designer;* John Conley, *Assistant*